Do You See the Goats and Pebbles?

Do You See the Goats and Pebbles?

BECKY NEALE

ILLUSTRATED BY
KEITH BABCOCK

Do You See the Goats and Pebbles?
The Do You See series by
Becky Neale

Published by Reading with Kids Press, St. Louis, MO
Copyright ©2022 Becky Neale
All rights reserved.

Project Management and Book Design: Davis Creative Publishing Partners, LLC / CreativePublishingPartners.com
Illustrator and Cover Design: Keith Babcock
Editor: Barb Maurer
Copyeditor: Barb Maurer

Names: Neale, Becky, author. | Babcock, Keith, illustrator.
Title: Do you see the goats and pebbles? / Becky Neale ; illustrated by Keith Babcock.
Description: St. Louis, MO : Reading with Kids Press, [2022] | Series: Do you see? | Interest age level: 000-012. | Summary: A goat herder matches up one pebble for every goat to make sure they are all home at night. When one pebble is without a goat, he has to go find the lost goat before it is too late.--Publisher.
Identifiers: ISBN: 978-1-955801-00-3 (paperback) | LCCN: 2022915635
Subjects: LCSH: Goatherds--Juvenile fiction. | Goats--Juvenile fiction. | Pebbles--Juvenile fiction. | Counting--Juvenile fiction. | CYAC: Herders--Fiction. | Goats--Fiction. | Pebbles--Fiction. | Lost and found possessions--Fiction. | Counting--Fiction. | LCGFT: Humorous fiction. | BISAC: JUVENILE FICTION / Animals / Farm Animals. | JUVENILE FICTION / Concepts / Counting & Numbers. | JUVENILE FICTION / Humorous Stories.
Classification: LCC: PZ7.1.N382 Do 2022 | DDC: [E]--dc23

ATTENTION CORPORATIONS, UNIVERSITIES, COLLEGES AND PROFESSIONAL ORGANIZATIONS: Quantity discounts are available on bulk purchases of this book for educational, gift purposes, or as premiums for increasing magazine subscriptions or renewals. Special books or book excerpts can also be created to fit specific needs. For information, please contact Becky Neale, Reading with Kids Press, readingwithkidspress proton.me, readingwithkidspress.com.

This book is dedicated to Parker Cummins.
Because of you my faith in God grew.

Dear Reader

This book takes place in the Middle East at some point between 10,000 and 3,000BC. During this time many animals and plants were in the process of being tamed and domesticated by humans.

I'd like to take a moment to tell you that goats do actually climb trees, and my illustrator has given one goat in particular the "super power" to climb not just with his hooves but also his jaws. This goat happens to be my favorite goat to watch.

Becky

Here are where the goats sleep.
Do you see any other creatures sleeping?

Do you see the spider?
I hope he makes his web soon. We may
see this spider again along with a snake
and butterfly.

Do you see all ten goats?
Can you find all of them?

Do you see them sleeping?
They sleep until the sun is up.

Do you see the sun?
It's rising behind us. Let's turn around.

Do you see the tree?
The sun is rising behind that tree and
will soon shine inside the shelter on
the goats.

Do you see the sun shining on the goats?
They are starting to wake up.

Do you see which goats are awake?
Can you point to them? Point gently so
you don't startle them. You can scratch
behind their ears if you like.
I know they like that.

Do you see the gate?
Let's go around and open it.

Do you see my pebbles?
Can you draw lines with your
finger from the pebbles to the goats?
Draw one line between each pebble
and goat. Be cautious, they may try to
bite your finger. Goats will nibble on
almost anything.

Does each pebble match to a goat?
Yes. We have the same amount of pebbles
as we have goats.

Do you see the goats playing?

Do you see the big horned goat eating?
It looks like he is eating grape vines.

Do you see the big horned goat jumping?
He left some grape vine leaves for us to investigate.

Do you see the grape vine leaves?
Each grape vine leaf has five points.
The points are called lobes.

Do you see the lobes?
Can you count five lobes on a leaf?

Do you see the big horned goat jumping
again?
Let's ask him where he's going.
"Where are you going big horned goat?
We see your tracks."

We could follow his tracks if you like.

14

Do you see the big horned goat yet?
No, but we can still see his tracks.

Do you see the big white goat?
Let's go back to the shelter and
check on the big white goat.
She looks ready to give birth.

Do you see the babies?
The big white goat gave birth to her kids.
Did you know that baby goats are
called kids?

Do you see the little brown goat?
He must be their dad.

Do you see any pebbles?
We need to collect two more pebbles since
we now have two more goats.

Do you see the evening shadows?
It's time for bed. Looks like the big white
goat and her kids went to bed early.

Do you see the bell?
Can you ring the bell to call all the
goats home?

Do you see all twelve goats sleeping?
Let's check to see if they're all here.
Can you draw a line from each
pebble to a goat?
Then we can place the pebbles in the
pouch if we have all twelve goats inside.
I think we are missing a goat, since there
are only eleven in here.

Do you see the big horned goat?
I don't see him either.
Will you come help me find him?

Do you know which way he went?
We would have seen him if he came
this way, so let's follow the tracks up
the hill again.

Do you see him?
He must have eaten so many bluebell
flowers that he fell asleep. Let's get him
home quickly before the mountain lion
sniffs him out.

Do you see the mountain lion?
Hurry up and open the gate for our big
horned goat before the mountain lion
decides to have goat for supper.

Do you see our big horned goat inside the shelter?

Do you see one last pebble?
You can match it to our big horned goat and then place the pebble in the pouch with the other pebbles.

Good night, sweet goats.
See you tomorrow.

Acknowledgments

Barb Maurer is 100% responsible for this book getting published. Thanks to her this book was always found when Becky thought it was lost.

Becky Neale writes children's books because her favorite thing to do with children is read books. As of today, August 6, 2022, she's currently reading The Tale of Despereaux by Kate deCamillo and recommends it for ages 7 and up. Check in with her website to find out what she's recently read with her children and how they rate the book: readingwithkidspress.com.

She also recognizes the overall good effects of spending time reading with children and recommends this for all adults. Be warned, reading with your children will make them like you more than if you didn't read to them, and they make want to hang out with you even when you're trying to read by yourself or even when you're trying to read with your husband.

But in the end, the laughing, snuggling, connecting, giggling, learning, thinking are always worth the time spent reading with children.

Activity Pages

It's your turn to
color your own goats.

Have fun!

37

41

www.ingramcontent.com/pod-product-compliance
Lightning Source LLC
Chambersburg PA
CBHW041524120626
46551CB00018B/2562